Old Times

Other Works by Harold Pinter Published by Grove Press

THE BIRTHDAY PARTY *and* THE ROOM
THE CARETAKER *and* THE DUMB WAITER
THREE PLAYS (THE COLLECTION; A SLIGHT ACHE;
   THE DWARFS)
THE HOMECOMING
THE LOVER, TEA PARTY, *and* THE BASEMENT
A NIGHT OUT, NIGHT SCHOOL, REVUE SKETCHES:
   EARLY PLAYS
MAC (A MEMOIR)
LANDSCAPE *and* SILENCE
FIVE SCREENPLAYS (THE SERVANT; THE PUMPKIN
   EATER; THE QUILLER MEMORANDUM [THE
   BERLIN MEMORANDUM]; ACCIDENT; THE
   GO-BETWEEN)
NO MAN'S LAND
COMPLETE WORKS: ONE (THE BIRTHDAY PARTY;
   THE ROOM; THE DUMB WAITER; A SLIGHT ACHE;
   A NIGHT OUT; THE BLACK AND WHITE; THE
   EXAMINATION)
COMPLETE WORKS: TWO (THE CARETAKER; NIGHT
   SCHOOL; THE DWARFS; THE COLLECTION; THE
   LOVER; FIVE REVUE SKETCHES [TROUBLE IN THE
   WORKS; THE BLACK AND WHITE; REQUEST STOP;
   LAST TO GO; SPECIAL OFFER])
THE PROUST SCREENPLAY: A LA RECHERCHE
   DU TEMPS PERDU

OLD TIMES

by

Harold Pinter

GROVE PRESS, INC. / NEW YORK

First Evergreen Edition 1973
Fifth Printing 1977
ISBN: 0-394-17761-4
Grove Press ISBN: 0-8021-4143-9
Library of Congress Catalog Card Number: 72-182581

Manufactured in the United States of America

Distributed by Random House, Inc., New York

GROVE PRESS, INC., 196 West Houston Street, New York, N.Y. 10014

To Peter Hall

ACKNOWLEDGEMENTS

The extracts from the songs *Lovely to Look At* (copyright 1935 Jerome Kern), *They Can't Take That Away From Me* (copyright 1937 Gershwin Publishing Corp.), *The Way You Look Tonight* (copyright 1937 Jerome Kern), *All The Things You Are, Are Mine* (copyright 1939 Chappell & Co. Inc.), *I Get A Kick Out Of You* (copyright 1934 Harms Inc.), *Smoke Gets In Your Eyes* (copyright 1933 Jerome Kern) are reproduced by permission of Chappell & Co. Ltd; that from *Blue Moon* (Rogers and Hart; copyright 1934 by Robbins Music Corporation New York, Robbins Music Corp. Limited of 35 Soho Square, London, W.1) is also reproduced by permission. The lines from *These Foolish Things* on pages 28/29 are reprinted by permission of the copyright owners Boosey & Hawkes Music Publishers Ltd.

Old Times was first presented by the Royal Shakespeare Company at the Aldwych Theatre, London, on 1st June, 1971, with the following cast:

DEELEY	Colin Blakely
KATE	Dorothy Tutin
ANNA	Vivien Merchant

All in their early forties

Directed by Peter Hall

A converted farmhouse

A long window up centre. Bedroom door up left.
Front door up right.

Spare modern furniture.
Two sofas. An armchair.

Autumn. Night.

ACT ONE

Light dim. Three figures discerned.

DEELEY *slumped in armchair, still.*
KATE *curled on a sofa, still.*
ANNA *standing at the window, looking out.*

Silence

Lights up on DEELEY *and* KATE, *smoking cigarettes.*

ANNA'S *figure remains still in dim light at the window.*

KATE

(*Reflectively.*) Dark.

Pause

DEELEY

Fat or thin?

KATE

Fuller than me. I think.

Pause

DEELEY

She was then?

KATE

I think so.

DEELEY

She may not be now.

Pause

Was she your best friend?

KATE

Oh, what does that mean?

DEELEY

What?

KATE

The word friend . . . when you look back . . . all that time.

DEELEY

Can't you remember what you felt?

Pause

KATE

It is a very long time.

DEELEY

But you remember her. She remembers you. Or why would she be coming here tonight?

KATE

I suppose because she remembers me.

Pause

DEELEY

Did you *think* of her as your best friend?

KATE

She was my only friend.

DEELEY

Your best and only.

KATE

My one and only.

Pause

If you have only one of something you can't say it's the best of anything.

DEELEY

Because you have nothing to compare it with?

KATE

Mmnn.

Pause

DEELEY

(*Smiling.*) She was incomparable.

KATE

Oh, I'm sure she wasn't.

Pause

KATE

DEELEY

I didn't know you had so few friends.

KATE

I had none. None at all. Except her.

DEELEY

Why her?

KATE

I don't know.

Pause

She was a thief. She used to steal things.

DEELEY

Who from?

KATE

Me.

DEELEY

What things?

KATE

Bits and pieces. Underwear.

DEELEY *chuckles*.

DEELEY

Will you remind her?

KATE

Oh . . . I don't think so.

Pause

DEELEY

Is that what attracted you to her?

KATE

What?

DEELEY

The fact that she was a thief.

KATE

No.

Pause

DEELEY

Are you looking forward to seeing her?

KATE

No.

DEELEY

I am. I shall be very interested.

KATE

In what?

DEELEY

In you. I'll be watching you.

KATE

Me? Why?

DEELEY

To see if she's the same person.

KATE

You think you'll find that out through me?

DEELEY

Definitely.

Pause

KATE

I hardly remember her. I've almost totally forgotten her.

Pause

DEELEY

Any idea what she drinks?

KATE

None.

DEELEY

She may be a vegetarian.

KATE

Ask her.

DEELEY

It's too late. You've cooked your casserole.

Pause

Why isn't she married? I mean, why isn't she bringing her husband?

KATE

Ask her.

DEELEY

Do I have to ask her everything?

KATE

Do you want me to ask your questions for you?

DEELEY

No. Not at all.

Pause

KATE

Of course she's married.

DEELEY

How do you know?

KATE

Everyone's married.

DEELEY

Then why isn't she bringing her husband?

KATE

Isn't she?

Pause

DEELEY

Did she mention a husband in her letter?

KATE

No.

DEELEY

What do you think he'd be like? I mean, what sort of man would she have married? After all, she was your best – your only – friend. You must have some idea. What kind of man would he be?

KATE

I have no idea.

DEELEY

Haven't you any curiosity?

KATE

You forget. I know her.

DEELEY

You haven't seen her for twenty years.

KATE

You've never seen her. There's a difference.

Pause

DEELEY

At least the casserole is big enough for four.

KATE

You said she was a vegetarian.

Pause

DEELEY

Did *she* have many friends?

KATE

Oh . . . the normal amount, I suppose.

DEELEY

Normal? What's normal? You had none.

KATE

One.

DEELEY

Is that normal?

Pause

She . . . had quite a lot of friends, did she?

KATE

Hundreds.

DEELEY

You met them?

KATE

Not all, I think. But after all, we were living together. There were visitors, from time to time. I met them.

DEELEY

Her visitors?

KATE

What?

DEELEY

Her visitors. Her friends. You had no friends.

KATE

Her friends, yes.

DEELEY

You met them.

Pause

(*Abruptly*.) You lived together?

KATE

Mmmnn?

DEELEY

You lived together?

KATE

Of course.

DEELEY

I didn't know that.

KATE

Didn't you?

DEELEY

You never told me that. I thought you just knew each other.

KATE

We did.

DEELEY

But in fact you lived with each other.

KATE

Of course we did. How else would she steal my underwear from me? In the street?

Pause

DEELEY

I knew you had shared with someone at one time . . .

Pause

But I didn't know it was her.

KATE

Of course it was.

Pause

DEELEY

Anyway, none of this matters.

ANNA *turns from the window, speaking, and moves down to them, eventually sitting on the second sofa.*

ANNA

Queuing all night, the rain, do you remember? my goodness, the Albert Hall, Covent Garden, what did we eat? to look back, half the night, to do things we loved, we were young then of course, but what stamina, and to work in the morning, and to a concert, or the opera, or the ballet, that night, you haven't forgotten? and then riding on top of the bus down Kensington High Street, and the bus conductors, and then dashing for the matches for the gasfire and then I suppose scrambled eggs, or did we? who cooked? both giggling and chattering, both huddling to the heat, then bed and sleeping, and all the hustle and bustle in the morning, rushing for the bus again for work, lunchtimes in Green Park, exchanging all our news, with our very own sandwiches, innocent girls, innocent secretaries, and then the night to come, and goodness knows what excitement in store, I mean the sheer expectation of it all, the looking-for-wardness of it all, and so poor, but to be poor and young, and a girl, in London then . . . and the cafés we found, almost private ones, weren't they? where artists and writers and sometimes actors collected, and others with dancers, we sat hardly breath-ing with our coffee, heads bent, so as not to be seen, so as not to disturb, so as not to distract, and listened and listened to all those words, all those cafés and all those people, creative un-doubtedly, and does it still exist I wonder? do you know? can you tell me?

Slight pause

DEELEY

We rarely get to London.

KATE *stands, goes to a small table and pours coffee from a pot.*

KATE

Yes, I remember.

She adds milk and sugar to one cup and takes it to ANNA. *She takes a black coffee to* DEELEY *and then sits with her own.*

DEELEY

(*to* ANNA.) Do you drink brandy?

ANNA

I would love some brandy.

DEELEY *pours brandy for all and hands the glasses. He remains standing with his own.*

ANNA

Listen. What silence. Is it always as silent?

DEELEY

It's quite silent here, yes. Normally.

Pause

You can hear the sea sometimes if you listen very carefully.

ANNA

How wise you were to choose this part of the world, and how
sensible and courageous of you both to stay permanently in
such a silence.

DEELEY

My work takes me away quite often, of course. But Kate stays
here.

ANNA

No one who lived here would want to go far. I would not want
to go far, I would be afraid of going far, lest when I returned
the house would be gone.

DEELEY

Lest?

ANNA

What?

DEELEY

The word lest. Haven't heard it for a long time.

Pause

KATE

Sometimes I walk to the sea. There aren't many people. It's a long beach.

Pause

ANNA

But I would miss London, nevertheless. But of course I was a girl in London. We were girls together.

DEELEY

I wish I had known you both then.

ANNA

Do you?

DEELEY

Yes.

DEELEY *pours more brandy for himself.*

ANNA

You have a wonderful casserole.

DEELEY

What?

ANNA

I mean wife. So sorry. A wonderful wife.

DEELEY

Ah.

ANNA

I was referring to the casserole. I was referring to your wife's
cooking.

DEELEY

You're not a vegetarian, then?

ANNA

No. Oh no.

DEELEY

Yes, you need good food in the country, substantial food, to
keep you going, all the air . . . you know.

Pause

KATE

Yes, I quite like those kind of things, doing it.

ANNA

What kind of things?

KATE

Oh, you know, that sort of thing.

Pause

DEELEY

Do you mean cooking?

KATE

All that thing.

ANNA

We weren't terribly elaborate in cooking, didn't have the time, but every so often dished up an incredibly enormous stew, guzzled the lot, and then more often than not sat up half the night reading Yeats.

Pause

(*To herself*.) Yes. Every so often. More often than not.

ANNA *stands, walks to the window.*

And the sky is so still.

Pause

Can you see that tiny ribbon of light? Is that the sea? Is that the horizon?

DEELEY

You live on a very different coast.

ANNA

Oh, very different. I live on a volcanic island.

DEELEY

I know it.

ANNA

Oh, do you?

DEELEY

I've been there.

Pause

ANNA

I'm so delighted to be here.

DEELEY

It's nice I know for Katey to see you. She hasn't many friends.

ANNA

She has you.

DEELEY

She hasn't made many friends, although there's been every opportunity for her to do so.

ANNA

Perhaps she has all she wants.

DEELEY

She lacks curiosity.

ANNA

Perhaps she's happy.

Pause

KATE

Are you talking about me?

DEELEY

Yes.

ANNA

She was always a dreamer.

DEELEY

She likes taking long walks. All that. You know. Raincoat on. Off down the lane, hands deep in pockets. All that kind of thing.

ANNA *turns to look at* KATE.

ANNA

Yes.

DEELEY

Sometimes I take her face in my hands and look at it.

ANNA

Really?

DEELEY

Yes, I look at it, holding it in my hands. Then I kind of let it go, take my hands away, leave it floating.

KATE

My head is quite fixed. I have it on.

DEELEY

(*To* ANNA.) It just floats away.

ANNA

She was always a dreamer.

ANNA *sits.*

Sometimes, walking, in the park, I'd say to her, you're dreaming, you're dreaming, wake up, what are you dreaming? and

she'd look round at me, flicking her hair, and look at me as if I
were part of her dream.

Pause

One day she said to me, I've slept through Friday. No you
haven't, I said, what do you mean? I've slept right through
Friday, she said. But today is Friday, I said, it's been Friday
all day, it's now Friday night, you haven't slept through Friday.
Yes I have, she said, I've slept right through it, today is
Saturday.

DEELEY

You mean she literally didn't know what day it was?

ANNA

No.

KATE

Yes I did. It was Saturday.

Pause

DEELEY

What month are we in?

KATE

September.

Pause

DEELEY

We're forcing her to think. We must see you more often.
You're a healthy influence.

ANNA

But she was always a charming companion.

DEELEY

Fun to live with?

ANNA

Delightful.

DEELEY

Lovely to look at, delightful to know.

ANNA

Ah, those songs. We used to play them, all of them, all the time, late at night, lying on the floor, lovely old things. Sometimes I'd look at her face, but she was quite unaware of my gaze.

DEELEY

Gaze?

ANNA

What?

DEELEY

The word gaze. Don't hear it very often.

ANNA

Yes, quite unaware of it. She was totally absorbed.

DEELEY

In Lovely to look at, delightful to know?

KATE

(*To* ANNA.) I don't know that song. Did we have it?

DEELEY

(*Singing,* to KATE.) You're lovely to look at, delightful to know . . .

ANNA

Oh we did. Yes, of course. We had them all.

DEELEY

(*Singing.*) Blue moon, I see you standing alone . . .

ANNA

(*Singing.*) The way you comb your hair . . .

DEELEY

(*Singing.*) Oh no they can't take that away from me . . .

ANNA

(*Singing.*) Oh but you're lovely, with your smile so warm . . .

DEELEY

(*Singing.*) I've got a woman crazy for me. She's funny that way.

Slight pause

ANNA

(*Singing.*) You are the promised kiss of springtime . . .

DEELEY

(*Singing.*) And someday I'll know that moment divine,
When all the things you are, are mine!

Slight pause

ANNA

(*Singing.*) I get no kick from champagne,
　　　　　Mere alcohol doesn't thrill me at all,
　　　　　So tell me why should it be true –

DEELEY

(*Singing.*) That I get a kick out of you?

Pause

ANNA

(*Singing.*) They asked me how I knew
　　　　　My true love was true,
　　　　　I of course replied,
　　　　　Something here inside
　　　　　Cannot be denied.

DEELEY

(*Singing.*) When a lovely flame dies . . .

ANNA

(*Singing.*) Smoke gets in your eyes.

Pause

DEELEY

(*Singing.*) The sigh of midnight trains in empty stations . . .

Pause

ANNA

(*Singing.*) The park at evening when the bell has sounded . . .

Pause

DEELEY

(*Singing.*) The smile of Garbo and the scent of roses . . .

ANNA

(*Singing.*) The waiters whistling as the last bar closes . . .

DEELEY

(*Singing.*) Oh, how the ghost of you clings . . .

Pause

They don't make them like that any more.

Silence

What happened to me was this. I popped into a fleapit to see
Odd Man Out. Some bloody awful summer afternoon, walking
in no direction. I remember thinking there was something
familiar about the neighbourhood and suddenly recalled that
it was in this very neighbourhood that my father bought me
my first tricycle, the only tricycle in fact I ever possessed. Anyway, there was the bicycle shop and there was this fleapit showing Odd Man Out and there were two usherettes standing in
the foyer and one of them was stroking her breasts and the
other one was saying 'dirty bitch' and the one stroking her
breasts was saying 'mmnnn' with a very sensual relish and
smiling at her fellow usherette, so I marched in on this ex-
cruciatingly hot summer afternoon in the middle of nowhere
and watched Odd Man Out and thought Robert Newton was
fantastic. And I still think he was fantastic. And I would
commit murder for him, even now. And there was only one
other person in the cinema, one other person in the whole of

the whole cinema, and there she is. And there she was, very dim, very still, placed more or less I would say at the dead centre of the auditorium. I was off centre and have remained so. And I left when the film was over, noticing, even though James Mason was dead, that the first usherette appeared to be utterly exhausted, and I stood for a moment in the sun, thinking I suppose about something and then this girl came out and I think looked about her and I said wasn't Robert Newton fantastic, and she said something or other, Christ knows what, but looked at me, and I thought Jesus this is it, I've made a catch, this is a trueblue pickup, and when we had sat down in the café with tea she looked into her cup and then up at me and told me she thought Robert Newton was remarkable. So it was Robert Newton who brought us together and it is only Robert Newton who can tear us apart.

Pause

ANNA

F. J. McCormick was good too.

DEELEY

I know F. J. McCormick was good too. But he didn't bring us together.

Pause

DEELEY

You've seen the film then?

ANNA

Yes.

DEELEY

When?

ANNA

Oh . . . long ago.

Pause

DEELEY

(*To* KATE.) Remember that film?

KATE

Oh yes. Very well.

Pause

DEELEY

I think I am right in saying the next time we met we held
hands. I held her cool hand, as she walked by me, and I said
something which made her smile, and she looked at me, didn't
you, flicking her hair back, and I thought she was even more
fantastic than Robert Newton.

Pause

And then at a slightly later stage our naked bodies met, hers
cool, warm, highly agreeable, and I wondered what Robert
Newton would think of this. What would he think of this I
wondered as I touched her profoundly all over.
(*To* ANNA.) What do you think he'd think?

ANNA

I never met Robert Newton but I do know I know what you
mean. There are some things one remembers even though they

may never have happened. There are things I remember which may never have happened but as I recall them so they take place.

DEELEY

What?

ANNA

This man crying in our room. One night late I returned and found him sobbing, his hand over his face, sitting in the armchair, all crumpled in the armchair and Katey sitting on the bed with a mug of coffee and no one spoke to me, no one spoke, no one looked up. There was nothing I could do. I undressed and switched out the light and got into my bed, the curtains were thin, the light from the street came in, Katey still, on her bed, the man sobbed, the light came in, it flicked the wall, there was a slight breeze, the curtains occasionally shook, there was nothing but sobbing, suddenly it stopped. The man came over to me, quickly, looked down at me, but I would have absolutely nothing to do with him, nothing.

Pause

No, no, I'm quite wrong . . . he didn't move quickly . . . that's quite wrong . . . he moved . . . very slowly, the light was bad, and stopped. He stood in the centre of the room. He looked at us both, at our beds. Then he turned towards me. He approached my bed. He bent down over me. But I would have nothing to do with him, absolutely nothing.

Pause

DEELEY

What kind of man was he?

ANNA

But after a while I heard him go out. I heard the front door close, and footsteps in the street, then silence, then the footsteps fade away, and then silence.

Pause

But then sometime later in the night I woke up and looked across the room to her bed and saw two shapes.

DEELEY

He'd come back!

ANNA

He was lying across her lap on her bed.

DEELEY

A man in the dark across my wife's lap?

Pause

ANNA

But then in the early morning . . . he had gone.

DEELEY

Thank Christ for that.

ANNA

It was as if he had never been.

DEELEY

Of course he'd been. He went twice and came once.

Pause

Well, what an exciting story that was.

Pause

What did he look like, this fellow?

ANNA

Oh, I never saw his face clearly. I don't know.

DEELEY

But was he – ?

KATE *stands. She goes to a small table, takes a cigarette from a box and lights it. She looks down at* ANNA.

KATE

You talk of me as if I were dead.

ANNA

No, no, you weren't dead, you were so lively, so animated, you used to laugh –

DEELEY

Of course you did. I made you smile myself, didn't I? walking along the street, holding hands. You smiled fit to bust.

ANNA

Yes, she could be so . . . animated.

DEELEY

Animated is no word for it. When she smiled . . . how can I describe it?

ANNA

Her eyes lit up.

DEELEY

I couldn't have put it better myself.

DEELEY *stands, goes to cigarette box, picks it up, smiles at* KATE.
KATE *looks at him, watches him light a cigarette, takes the box
from him, crosses to* ANNA, *offers her a cigarette.* ANNA *takes one.*

ANNA

You weren't dead. Ever. In any way.

KATE

I said you talk about me as if I *am* dead. Now.

ANNA

How can you say that? How can you say that, when I'm looking
at you now, seeing you so shyly poised over me, looking down
at me –

DEELEY

Stop that!

Pause

KATE *sits.*
DEELEY *pours a drink.*

DEELEY

Myself I was a student then, juggling with my future, wonder-
ing should I bejasus saddle myself with a slip of a girl not long
out of her swaddling clothes whose only claim to virtue was
silence but who lacked any sense of fixedness, any sense of
decisiveness, but was compliant only to the shifting winds,
with which she went, but not *the* winds, and certainly not my
winds, such as they are, but I suppose winds that only she

understood, and that of course with no understanding whatso-
ever, at least as I understand the word, at least that's the way I
figured it. A classic female figure, I said to myself, or is it a
classic female posture, one way or the other long outworn.

Pause

That's the position as I saw it then. I mean, that is my cate-
gorical pronouncement on the position as I saw it then. Twenty
years ago.

Silence

ANNA

When I heard that Katey was married my heart leapt with joy.

DEELEY

How did the news reach you?

ANNA

From a friend.

Pause

Yes, it leapt with joy. Because you see I knew she never did
things loosely or carelessly, recklessly. Some people throw a
stone into a river to see if the water's too cold for jumping,
others, a few others, will always wait for the ripples before they
will jump.

DEELEY

Some people do *what*? (*To* KATE.) What did she say?

ANNA

And I knew that Katey would always wait not just for the first
emergence of ripple but for the ripples to pervade and pervade

the surface, for of course as you know ripples on the surface indicate a shimmering in depth down through every particle of water down to the river bed, but even when she felt that happen, when she was assured it was happening, she still might not jump. But in this case she did jump and I knew therefore she had fallen in love truly and was glad. And I deduced it must also have happened to you.

DEELEY

You mean the ripples?

ANNA

If you like.

DEELEY

Do men ripple too?

ANNA

Some, I would say.

DEELEY

I see.

Pause

ANNA

And later when I found out the kind of man you were I was doubly delighted because I knew Katey had always been interested in the arts.

KATE

I was interested once in the arts, but I can't remember now which ones they were.

ANNA

Don't tell me you've forgotten our days at the Tate? and how
we explored London and all the old churches and all the old
buildings, I mean those that were left from the bombing, in the
City and south of the river in Lambeth and Greenwich? Oh
my goodness. Oh yes. And the Sunday papers! I could never
get her away from the review pages. She ravished them, and
then insisted we visit that gallery, or this theatre, or that
chamber concert, but of course there was so much, so much to
see and to hear, in lovely London then, that sometimes we
missed things, or had no more money, and so missed some
things. For example, I remember one Sunday she said to me,
looking up from the paper, come quick, quick, come with me
quickly, and we seized our handbags and went, on a bus, to
some totally obscure, some totally unfamiliar district and,
almost alone, saw a wonderful film called Odd Man Out.

Silence

DEELEY

Yes, I do quite a bit of travelling in my job.

ANNA

Do you enjoy it?

DEELEY

Enormously. Enormously.

ANNA

Do you go far?

DEELEY

I travel the globe in my job.

ANNA

And poor Katey when you're away? What does she do?

ANNA *looks at* KATE.

KATE

Oh, I continue.

ANNA

Is he away for long periods?

KATE

I think, sometimes. Are you?

ANNA

You leave your wife for such long periods? How can you?

DEELEY

I have to do a lot of travelling in my job.

ANNA

(*To* KATE.) I think I must come and keep you company when he's away.

DEELEY

Won't your husband miss you?

ANNA

Of course. But he would understand.

DEELEY

Does he understand now?

ANNA

Of course.

DEELEY

We had a vegetarian dish prepared for him.

ANNA

He's not a vegetarian. In fact he's something of a gourmet. We live in a rather fine villa and have done so for many years. It's very high up, on the cliffs.

DEELEY

You eat well up there, eh?

ANNA

I would say so, yes.

DEELEY

Yes, I know Sicily slightly. Just slightly. Taormina. Do you live in Taormina?

ANNA

Just outside.

DEELEY

Just outside, yes. Very high up. Yes, I've probably caught a glimpse of your villa.

Pause

My work took me to Sicily. My work concerns itself with life all over, you see, in every part of the globe. With people all over the globe. I use the word globe because the word world possesses emotional political sociological and psychological pretensions and resonances which I prefer as a matter of choice

to do without, or shall I say to steer clear of, or if you like to
reject. How's the yacht?

ANNA

Oh, very well.

DEELEY

Captain steer a straight course?

ANNA

As straight as we wish, when we wish it.

DEELEY

Don't you find England damp, returning?

ANNA

Rather beguilingly so.

DEELEY

Rather beguilingly so? (*To himself.*) What the hell does she mean
by that?

Pause

Well, any time your husband finds himself in this direction my
little wife will be only too glad to put the old pot on the old gas
stove and dish him up something luscious if not voluptuous.
No trouble.

Pause

I suppose his business interests kept him from making the trip.
What's his name? Gian Carlo or Per Paulo?

KATE

(*To* ANNA.) Do you have marble floors?

ANNA

Yes.

KATE

Do you walk in bare feet on them?

ANNA

Yes. But I wear sandals on the terrace, because it can be rather severe on the soles.

KATE

The sun, you mean? The heat.

ANNA

Yes.

DEELEY

I had a great crew in Sicily. A marvellous cameraman. Irving Shultz. Best in the business. We took a pretty austere look at the women in black. The little old women in black. I wrote the film and directed it. My name is Orson Welles.

KATE

(*To* ANNA.) Do you drink orange juice on your terrace in the morning, and bullshots at sunset, and look down at the sea?

ANNA

Sometimes, yes.

DEELEY

As a matter of fact I am at the top of my profession, as a matter of fact, and I have indeed been associated with substantial numbers of articulate and sensitive people, mainly prostitutes of all kinds.

KATE

(*To* ANNA.) And do you like the Sicilian people?

DEELEY

I've been there. There's nothing more to see, there's nothing more to investigate, nothing. There's nothing more in Sicily to investigate.

KATE

(*To* ANNA.) Do you like the Sicilian people?

ANNA *stares at her.*

Silence

ANNA

(*Quietly.*) Don't let's go out tonight, don't let's go anywhere tonight, let's stay in. I'll cook something, you can wash your hair, you can relax, we'll put on some records.

KATE

Oh, I don't know. We could go out.

ANNA

Why do you want to go out?

KATE

We could walk across the park.

ANNA

The park is dirty at night, all sorts of horrible people, men hiding behind trees and women with terrible voices, they scream at you as you go past, and people come out suddenly

from behind trees and bushes and there are shadows every-
where and there are policemen, and you'll have a horrible
walk, and you'll see all the traffic and the noise of the traffic and
you'll see all the hotels, and you know you hate looking
through all those swing doors, you hate it, to see all that, all
those people in the lights in the lobbies all talking and moving
. . . and all the chandeliers . . .

Pause

You'll only want to come home if you go out. You'll want to
run home . . . and into your room. . . .

Pause

KATE

What shall we do then?

ANNA

Stay in. Shall I read to you? Would you like that?

KATE

I don't know.

Pause

ANNA

Are you hungry?

KATE

No.

DEELEY

Hungry? After that casserole?

Pause

KATE

What shall I wear tomorrow? I can't make up my mind.

ANNA

Wear your green.

KATE

I haven't got the right top.

ANNA

You have. You have your turquoise blouse.

KATE

Do they go?

ANNA

Yes, they do go. Of course they go.

KATE

I'll try it.

Pause

ANNA

Would you like me to ask someone over?

KATE

Who?

ANNA

Charley . . . or Jake?

KATE

I don't like Jake.

ANNA

Well, Charley . . . or . . .

KATE

Who?

ANNA

McCabe.

Pause

KATE

I'll think about it in the bath.

ANNA

Shall I run your bath for you?

KATE

(*Standing.*) No. I'll run it myself tonight.

KATE *slowly walks to the bedroom door, goes out, closes it.*

DEELEY *stands looking at* ANNA.
ANNA *turns her head towards him.*

They look at each other.

FADE

ACT TWO

The bedroom.
A long window up centre. Door to bathroom up left. Door to sitting-room up right.

Two divans. An armchair.

The divans and armchair are disposed in precisely the same relation to each other as the furniture in the first act, but in reversed positions.

Lights dim. ANNA *discerned sitting on divan. Faint glow from glass panel in bathroom door.*

Silence.

Lights up. The other door opens. DEELEY *comes in with tray.*

DEELEY *comes into the room, places the tray on a table.*

DEELEY
Here we are. Good and hot. Good and strong and hot. You prefer it white with sugar, I believe?

ANNA
Please.

DEELEY

(*Pouring.*) Good and strong and hot with white and sugar.

He hands her the cup.

Like the room?

ANNA

Yes.

DEELEY

We sleep here. These are beds. The great thing about these beds is that they are susceptible to any amount of permutation. They can be separated as they are now. Or placed at right angles, or one can bisect the other, or you can sleep feet to feet, or head to head, or side by side. It's the castors that make all this possible.

He sits with coffee.

Yes, I remember you quite clearly from The Wayfarers.

ANNA

The what?

DEELEY

The Wayfarers Tavern, just off the Brompton Road.

ANNA

When was that?

DEELEY

Years ago.

ANNA

I don't think so.

DEELEY

Oh yes, it was you, no question. I never forget a face. You sat in
the corner, quite often, sometimes alone, sometimes with
others. And here you are, sitting in my house in the country.
The same woman. Incredible. Fellow called Luke used to go
in there. You knew him.

ANNA

Luke?

DEELEY

Big chap. Ginger hair. Ginger beard.

ANNA

I don't honestly think so.

DEELEY

Yes, a whole crowd of them, poets, stunt men, jockeys, stand-
up comedians, that kind of setup. You used to wear a scarf,
that's right, a black scarf, and a black sweater, and a skirt.

ANNA

Me?

DEELEY

And black stockings. Don't tell me you've forgotten The Wayfarers Tavern? You might have forgotten the name but you
must remember the pub. You were the darling of the saloon
bar.

ANNA

I wasn't rich, you know. I didn't have money for alcohol.

DEELEY

You had escorts. You didn't have to pay. You were looked after.
I bought you a few drinks myself.

ANNA

You?

DEELEY

Sure.

ANNA

Never.

DEELEY

It's the truth. I remember clearly.

Pause

ANNA

You?

DEELEY

I've bought you drinks.

Pause

Twenty years ago . . . or so.

ANNA

You're saying we've met before?

DEELEY

Of course we've met before.

Pause

We've talked before. In that pub, for example. In the corner.
Luke didn't like it much but we ignored him. Later we all went
to a party. Someone's flat, somewhere in Westbourne Grove.
You sat on a very low sofa, I sat opposite and looked up your
skirt. Your black stockings were very black because your
thighs were so white. That's something that's all over now, of
course, isn't it, nothing like the same palpable profit in it now,
it's all over. But it was worthwhile then. It was worthwhile
that night. I simply sat sipping my light ale and gazed . . .
gazed up your skirt. You didn't object, you found my gaze
perfectly acceptable.

ANNA

I was aware of your gaze, was I?

DEELEY

There was a great argument going on, about China or something, or death, or China *and* death, I can't remember which,
but nobody but I had a thigh-kissing view, nobody but you had
the thighs which kissed. And here you are. Same woman.
Same thighs.

Pause

Yes. Then a friend of yours came in, a girl, a girl friend. She
sat on the sofa with you, you both chatted and chuckled, sitting
together, and I settled lower to gaze at you both, at both your
thighs, squealing and hissing, you aware, she unaware, but
then a great multitude of men surrounded me, and demanded
my opinion about death, or about China, or whatever it was,
and they would not let me be but bent down over me, so that
what with their stinking breath and their broken teeth and the
hair in their noses and China and death and their arses on the
arms of my chair I was forced to get up and plunge my way
through them, followed by them with ferocity, as if I were the

cause of their argument, looking back through smoke, rushing to the table with the linoleum cover to look for one more full bottle of light ale, looking back through smoke, glimpsing two girls on the sofa, one of them you, heads close, whispering, no longer able to see anything, no longer able to see stocking or thigh, and then you were gone. I wandered over to the sofa. There was no one on it. I gazed at the indentations of four buttocks. Two of which were yours.

Pause

ANNA

I've rarely heard a sadder story.

DEELEY

I agree.

ANNA

I'm terribly sorry.

DEELEY

That's all right.

Pause

I never saw you again. You disappeared from the area. Perhaps you moved out.

ANNA

No. I didn't.

DEELEY

I never saw you in The Wayfarers Tavern again. Where were you?

ANNA

Oh, at concerts, I should think, or the ballet.

Silence

Katey's taking a long time over her bath.

DEELEY

Well, you know what she's like when she gets in the bath.

ANNA

Yes.

DEELEY

Enjoys it. Takes a long time over it.

ANNA

She does, yes.

DEELEY

A hell of a long time. Luxuriates in it. Gives herself a great soaping all over.

Pause

Really soaps herself all over, and then washes the soap off, sud by sud. Meticulously. She's both thorough and, I must say it, sensuous. Gives herself a comprehensive going over, and apart from everything else she does emerge as clean as a new pin. Don't you think?

ANNA

Very clean.

DEELEY

Truly so. Not a speck. Not a tidemark. Shiny as a balloon.

ANNA

Yes, a kind of floating.

DEELEY

What?

ANNA

She floats from the bath. Like a dream. Unaware of anyone standing, with her towel, waiting for her, waiting to wrap it round her. Quite absorbed.

Pause

Until the towel is placed on her shoulders.

Pause

DEELEY

Of course she's so totally incompetent at drying herself properly, did you find that? She gives herself a really good *scrub*, but can she with the same efficiency give herself an equally good *rub*? I have found, in my experience of her, that this is not in fact the case. You'll always find a few odd unexpected unwanted cheeky globules dripping about.

ANNA

Why don't you dry her yourself?

DEELEY

Would you recommend that?

ANNA

You'd do it properly.

DEELEY

In her bath towel?

ANNA

How out?

DEELEY

How out?

ANNA

How could you dry her out? Out of her bath towel?

DEELEY

I don't know.

ANNA

Well, dry her yourself, in her bath towel.

Pause

DEELEY

Why don't *you* dry her in her bath towel?

ANNA

Me?

DEELEY

You'd do it properly.

ANNA

No, no.

DEELEY

Surely? I mean, you're a woman, you know how and where and in what density moisture collects on women's bodies.

ANNA

No two women are the same.

DEELEY

Well, that's true enough.

Pause

I've got a brilliant idea. Why don't we do it with powder?

ANNA

Is that a brilliant idea?

DEELEY

Isn't it?

ANNA

It's quite common to powder yourself after a bath.

DEELEY

It's quite common to powder yourself after a bath but it's quite uncommon to be powdered. Or is it? It's not common where I come from, I can tell you. My mother would have a fit.

Pause

Listen. I'll tell you what. I'll do it. I'll do the whole lot. The towel and the powder. After all, I am her husband. But you can supervise the whole thing. And give me some hot tips while you're at it. That'll kill two birds with one stone.

Pause

(*To himself.*) Christ.

He looks at her slowly.

You must be about forty, I should think, by now.

Pause

If I walked into The Wayfarers Tavern now, and saw you sitting in the corner, I wouldn't recognize you.

The bathroom door opens. KATE *comes into the bedroom. She wears a bathrobe.*

She smiles at DEELEY *and* ANNA.

KATE

(*With pleasure.*) Aaahh.

She walks to the window and looks out into the night. DEELEY *and* ANNA *watch her.*

DEELEY *begins to sing softly.*

DEELEY

(*Singing.*) The way you wear your hat . . .

ANNA

(*Singing, softly.*) The way you sip your tea . . .

DEELEY

(*Singing*.) The memory of all that . . .

ANNA

(*Singing*.) No, no, they can't take that away from me . . .

KATE *turns from the window to look at them.*

ANNA

(*Singing*.) The way your smile just beams . . .

DEELEY

(*Singing*.) The way you sing off key . . .

ANNA

(*Singing*.) The way you haunt my dreams . . .

DEELEY

(*Singing*.) No, no, they can't take that away from me . . .

KATE *walks down towards them and stands, smiling.* ANNA *and*
DEELEY *sing again, faster on cue, and more perfunctorily.*

ANNA

(*Singing*.) The way you hold your knife –

DEELEY

(*Singing*.) The way we danced till three –

ANNA

(*Singing*.) The way you've changed my life –

DEELEY

No, no, they can't take that away from me.

KATE *sits on a divan.*

ANNA

(*To* DEELEY.) Doesn't she look beautiful?

DEELEY

Doesn't she?

KATE

Thank you. I feel fresh. The water's very soft here. Much softer than London. I always find the water very hard in London. That's one reason I like living in the country. Everything's softer. The water, the light, the shapes, the sounds. There aren't such edges here. And living close to the sea too. You can't say where it begins or ends. That appeals to me. I don't care for harsh lines. I deplore that kind of urgency. I'd like to go to the East, or somewhere like that, somewhere very hot, where you can lie under a mosquito net and breathe quite slowly. You know . . . somewhere where you can look through the flap of a tent and see sand, that kind of thing. The only nice thing about a big city is that when it rains it blurs everything, and it blurs the lights from the cars, doesn't it, and blurs your eyes, and you have rain on your lashes. That's the only nice thing about a big city.

ANNA

That's not the only nice thing. You can have a nice room and a nice gas fire and a warm dressing gown and a nice hot drink, all waiting for you for when you come in.

Pause

KATE

Is it raining?

ANNA

No.

KATE

Well, I've decided I will stay in tonight anyway.

ANNA

Oh good. I am glad. Now you can have a good strong cup of coffee after your bath.

ANNA *stands, goes to coffee, pours.*

I could do the hem on your black dress. I could finish it and you could try it on.

KATE

Mmmnn.

ANNA *hands her her coffee.*

ANNA

Or I could read to you.

DEELEY

Have you dried yourself properly, Kate?

KATE

I think so.

DEELEY

Are you sure? All over?

KATE

I think so. I feel quite dry.

DEELEY

Are you quite sure? I don't want you sitting here damply all
over the place.

KATE *smiles.*

See that smile? That's the same smile she smiled when I was
walking down the street with her, after Odd Man Out, well,
quite some time after.
What did you think of it?

ANNA

It is a very beautiful smile.

DEELEY

Do it again.

KATE

I'm still smiling.

DEELEY

You're not. Not like you were a moment ago, not like you did
then.

(*To* ANNA.) You know the smile I'm talking about?

KATE

This coffee's cold.

Pause

ANNA

Oh, I'm sorry. I'll make some fresh.

KATE

No, I don't want any, thank you.

Pause

Is Charley coming?

ANNA

I can ring him if you like.

KATE

What about McCabe?

ANNA

Do you really want to see anyone?

KATE

I don't think I like McCabe.

ANNA

Nor do I.

KATE

He's strange. He says some very strange things to me.

ANNA

What things?

KATE

Oh, all sorts of funny things.

ANNA

I've never liked him.

KATE

Duncan's nice though, isn't he?

ANNA

Oh yes.

KATE

I like his poetry so much.

Pause

But you know who I like best?

ANNA

Who?

KATE

Christy.

ANNA

He's lovely.

KATE

He's so gentle, isn't he? And his humour. Hasn't he got a lovely
sense of humour? And I think he's . . . so sensitive. Why don't
you ask him round?

DEELEY

He can't make it. He's out of town.

KATE

Oh, what a pity.

Silence

DEELEY

(*To* ANNA.) Are you intending to visit anyone else while you're in England? Relations? Cousins? Brothers?

ANNA

No. I know no one. Except Kate.

Pause

DEELEY

Do you find her changed?

ANNA

Oh, just a little, not very much. (*To* KATE.) You're still shy, aren't you?

KATE *stares at her.*

(*To* DEELEY.) But when I knew her first she was *so* shy, as shy as a fawn, she really was. When people leaned to speak to her she would fold away from them, so that though she was still standing within their reach she was no longer accessible to them. She folded herself from them, they were no longer able to speak or go through with their touch. I put it down to her upbringing, a parson's daughter, and indeed there was a good deal of Brontë about her.

DEELEY

Was she a parson's daughter?

ANNA

But if I thought Brontë I did not think she was Brontë in passion but only in secrecy, in being so stubbornly private.

Slight pause

I remember her first blush.

DEELEY

What? What was it? I mean why was it?

ANNA

I had borrowed some of her underwear, to go to a party. Later
that night I confessed. It was naughty of me. She stared at me,
nonplussed, perhaps, is the word. But I told her that in fact
I had been punished for my sin, for a man at the party had
spent the whole evening looking up my skirt.

Pause

DEELEY

She blushed at that?

ANNA

Deeply.

DEELEY

Looking up *your* skirt in *her* underwear. Mmnn.

ANNA

But from that night she insisted, from time to time, that I
borrow her underwear – she had more of it than I, and a far
greater range – and each time she proposed this she would
blush, but propose it she did, nevertheless. And when there
was anything to tell her, when I got back, anything of interest
to tell her, I told her.

DEELEY

Did she blush then?

ANNA

I could never see then. I would come in late and find her reading under the lamp, and begin to tell her, but she would say no,

turn off the light, and I would tell her in the dark. She preferred to be told in the dark. But of course it was never completely dark, what with the light from the gasfire or the light through the curtains, and what she didn't know was that, knowing her preference, I would choose a position in the room from which I could see her face, although she could not see mine. She could hear my voice only. And so she listened and I watched her listening.

DEELEY

Sounds a perfect marriage.

ANNA

We were great friends.

Pause

DEELEY

You say she was Brontë in secrecy but not in passion. What was she in passion?

ANNA

I feel that is your province.

DEELEY

You feel it's my province? Well, you're damn right. It is my province. I'm glad someone's showing a bit of taste at last. Of course it's my bloody province. I'm her husband.

Pause

I mean I'd like to ask a question. Am I alone in beginning to find all this distasteful?

ANNA

But what can you possibly find distasteful? I've flown from
Rome to see my oldest friend, after twenty years, and to meet
her husband. What is it that worries you?

DEELEY

What worries me is the thought of your husband rumbling
about alone in his enormous villa living hand to mouth on a
few hardboiled eggs and unable to speak a damn word of
English.

ANNA

I interpret, when necessary.

DEELEY

Yes, but you're here, with us. He's there, alone, lurching up
and down the terrace, waiting for a speedboat, waiting for a
speedboat to spill out beautiful people, at least. Beautiful
Mediterranean people. Waiting for all *that*, a kind of elegance
we know nothing about, a slim-bellied Cote d'Azur thing we
know absolutely nothing about, a lobster and lobster sauce
ideology we know fuck all about, the longest legs in the world,
the most phenomenally soft voices. I can hear them now. I
mean let's put it on the table, I have my eye on a number of
pulses, pulses all round the globe, deprivations and insults,
why should I waste valuable space listening to two –

KATE

(*Swiftly.*) If you don't like it go.

Pause

DEELEY

Go? Where can I go?

KATE

To China. Or Sicily.

DEELEY

I haven't got a speedboat. I haven't got a white dinner jacket.

KATE

China then.

DEELEY

You know what they'd do to me in China if they found me in a white dinner jacket. They'd bloodywell kill me. You know what they're like over there.

Slight pause

ANNA

You are welcome to come to Sicily at any time, both of you, and be my guests.

Silence

KATE *and* DEELEY *stare at her.*

ANNA

(*To* DEELEY, *quietly.*) I would like you to understand that I came here not to disrupt but to celebrate.

Pause

To celebrate a very old and treasured friendship, something that was forged between us long before you knew of our existence.

Pause

I found her. She grew to know wonderful people, through my introduction. I took her to cafés, almost private ones, where artists and writers and sometimes actors collected, and others with dancers, and we sat hardly breathing with our coffee, listening to the life around us. All I wanted for her was her happiness. That is all I want for her still.

Pause

DEELEY

(*To* KATE.) We've met before, you know. Anna and I.

KATE *looks at him.*

Yes, we met in the Wayfarers Tavern. In the corner. She took a fancy to me. Of course I was slimhipped in those days. Pretty nifty. A bit squinky, quite honestly. Curly hair. The lot. We had a scene together. She freaked out. She didn't have any bread, so I bought her a drink. She looked at me with big eyes, shy, all that bit. She was pretending to be you at the time. Did it pretty well. Wearing your underwear she was too, at the time. Amiably allowed me a gander. Trueblue generosity. Admirable in a woman. We went to a party. Given by philosophers. Not a bad bunch. Edgware road gang. Nice lot. Haven't seen any of them for years. Old friends. Always thinking. Spoke their thoughts. Those are the people I miss. They're all dead, anyway I've never seen them again. The Maida Vale group. Big Eric and little Tony. They lived somewhere near Paddington library. On the way to the party I took her into a café, bought her a cup of coffee, beards with faces. She thought she was you, said little, so little. Maybe she was you. Maybe it was you, having coffee with me, saying little, so little.

Pause

KATE

What do you think attracted her to you?

DEELEY

I don't know. What?

KATE

She found your face very sensitive, vulnerable.

DEELEY

Did she?

KATE

She wanted to comfort it, in the way only a woman can.

DEELEY

Did she?

KATE

Oh yes.

DEELEY

She wanted to comfort my face, in the way only a woman can?

KATE

She was prepared to extend herself to you.

DEELEY

I beg your pardon?

KATE

She fell in love with you.

DEELEY

With me?

KATE

You were so unlike the others. We knew men who were
brutish, crass.

DEELEY

There really are such men, then? Crass men?

KATE

Quite crass.

DEELEY

But I was crass, wasn't I, looking up her skirt?

KATE

That's not crass.

DEELEY

If it was her skirt. If it was her.

ANNA

(*Coldly.*) Oh, it was my skirt. It was me. I remember your look
. . . very well. I remember you well.

KATE

(*To* ANNA.) But I remember you. I remember you dead.

Pause

I remember you lying dead. You didn't know I was watching
you. I leaned over you. Your face was dirty. You lay dead, your

face scrawled with dirt, all kinds of earnest inscriptions, but unblotted, so that they had run, all over your face, down to your throat. Your sheets were immaculate. I was glad. I would have been unhappy if your corpse had lain in an unwholesome sheet. It would have been graceless. I mean as far as I was concerned. As far as my room was concerned. After all, you were dead in my room. When you woke my eyes were above you, staring down at you. You tried to do my little trick, one of my tricks you had borrowed, my little slow smile, my little slow shy smile, my bend of the head, my half closing of the eyes, that we knew so well, but it didn't work, the grin only split the dirt at the sides of your mouth and stuck. You stuck in your grin. I looked for tears but could see none. Your pupils weren't in your eyes. Your bones were breaking through your face. But all was serene. There was no suffering. It had all happened elsewhere. Last rites I did not feel necessary. Or any celebration. I felt the time and season appropriate and that by dying alone and dirty you had acted with proper decorum. It was time for my bath. I had quite a lengthy bath, got out, walked about the room, glistening, drew up a chair, sat naked beside you and watched you.

Pause

When I brought him into the room your body of course had gone. What a relief it was to have a different body in my room, a male body behaving quite differently, doing all those things they do and which they think are good, like sitting with one leg over the arm of an armchair. We had a choice of two beds. Your bed or my bed. To lie in, or on. To grind noses together, in or on. He liked your bed, and thought he was different in it because he was a man. But one night I said let me do something, a little thing, a little trick. He lay there in your bed. He looked up at me with great expectation. He was gratified. He thought I had profited from his teaching. He thought I was going to be sexually forthcoming, that I was about to take a long promised initiative. I dug about in the windowbox, where you had planted our pretty pansies, scooped, filled the bowl, and plastered his face with dirt. He resisted . . . with force. He would not let me dirty his face, or smudge it, he wouldn't let me. He suggested a wedding instead, and a change of environment.

Slight pause

Neither mattered.

Pause

He asked me once, at about that time, who had slept in that bed before him. I told him no one. No one at all.

Long silence

ANNA *stands, walks towards the door, stops, her back to them.*

Silence

DEELEY *starts to sob, very quietly.*

ANNA *stands still.*

ANNA *turns, switches off the lamps, sits on her divan, and lies down.*

The sobbing stops

Silence

DEELEY *stands. He walks a few paces, looks at both divans.*

He goes to ANNA'S *divan, looks down at her. She is still.*

Silence

DEELEY *moves towards the door, stops, his back to them.*

Silence

DEELEY *turns. He goes towards* KATE'S *divan. He sits on her divan, lies across her lap.*

Long silence

DEELEY *very slowly sits up.*
He gets off the divan.
He walks slowly to the armchair.
He sits, slumped.

Silence

Lights up full sharply. Very bright.

DEELEY *in armchair.*
ANNA *lying on divan.*
KATE *sitting on divan.*

Selected List of Grove Press
Drama and Theater Paperbacks

E471 BECKETT, SAMUEL / Cascando and Other Short Dramatic
      Pieces (Words and Music, Film, Play, Come and Go, Eh Joe,
      Endgame) / $1.95

E96 BECKETT, SAMUEL / Endgame / $1.95

E318 BECKETT, SAMUEL / Happy Days / $2.45

E226 BECKETT, SAMUEL / Krapp's Last Tape, plus All That Fall,
      Embers, Act Without Words I and II / $2.45

E33 BECKETT, SAMUEL / Waiting For Godot / $1.95 [See also
      Seven Plays of the Modern Theater, Harold Clurman, ed.
      GT422 / $4.95]

B117 BRECHT, BERTOLT / The Good Woman of Setzuan / $1.95

B108 BRECHT, BERTOLT / Mother Courage and Her
      Children / $1.50

B333 BRECHT, BERTOLT / The Threepenny Opera / $1.45

E130 GENET, JEAN / The Balcony / $2.95 [See also Seven Plays
      of the Modern Theater, Harold Clurman, ed. GT422 / $4.95]

E208 GENET, JEAN / The Blacks: A Clown Show / $2.95

E577 GENET, JEAN / The Maids and Deathwatch:
      Two Plays / $2.95

E374 GENET, JEAN / The Screens / $1.95

E101 IONESCO, EUGENE / Four Plays (The Bald Soprano, The
      Lesson, The Chairs,* Jack, or The Submission) / $1.95
      *[See also Eleven Short Plays of the Modern Theater,
      Samuel Moon, ed. B107 / $2.45]

E259 IONESCO, EUGENE / Rhinoceros* and Other Plays (The
      Leader, The Future is in Eggs, or It Takes All Sorts to Make
      a World) / $1.95 *[See also Seven Plays of the Modern
      Theater, Harold Clurman, ed. GT422 / $4.95]

E119 IONESCO, EUGENE / Three Plays (Amédée, The New
      Tenant, Victims of Duty) / $2.95

B354 PINTER, HAROLD / Old Times / $1.95

E299 PINTER, HAROLD / The Caretaker* and The Dumb Waiter:
      Two Plays / $1.95 *[See also Modern British Drama,
      Henry Popkin, ed. GT422 / $5.95]

E411 PINTER, HAROLD / The Homecoming / $1.95

E626 STOPPARD, TOM / Jumpers / $1.95

B319 STOPPARD, TOM / Rosencrantz and Guilderstern Are
      Dead / $1.95

GROVE PRESS, INC., 196 West Houston St., New York, N.Y. 10014